Christian Disciplines

CREATING TIME AND SPACE FOR GOD

I0806575

BEACON HILL PRESS
OF KANSAS CITY

Christian Disciplines

CREATING TIME AND SPACE FOR GOD

Editor
Mike L. Wonch
Director of Curriculum
Merritt J. Nielson
Director of Editorial
Bonnie Perry
Writer
Douglas S. Hardy

ISBN: 978-0-8341-2980-1
Printed in U.S.A.

10 9 8 7 6 5 4

CONTENTS

The God of love has captured my heart. It started when I was young and growing up in the church. Through their example and instruction, my community of faith nurtured in me a love for God and for people. The notion of Christianity as a practiced faith got into my bones. Then my denomination's youth magazine helped put spiritual flesh on those bones through a year-long series on the disciplines of the Christian life. Each monthly issue featured a different practice with guidance for how to incorporate it into life. That year proved to be a turning point for me, helping turn my desire to follow Christ into a way of living. My hope is that this study will be that kind of a resource for you.

Each chapter has been informed by the Bible—particularly the life and practices of Jesus—and by the teaching and example of John Wesley—the theological father of the Holiness tradition. I thank God for this heritage. I also want to thank the churches in Kansas City, USA; Moncton, Canada; and Ongata Rongai, Kenya, for invaluable help in the preparation of this study. You remind me that Christian disciplines are best learned and practiced in community. Thank you for being a means of grace to me.

Douglas S. Hardy

Dr. Doug Hardy serves as Professor of Spiritual Formation and Director of the Doctor of Ministry Program at Nazarene Theological Seminary in Kansas City, MO where he helps students who are preparing for pastoral ministry to pray as they learn. He grew up in Canada; studied, pastored, and taught in the United States; and recently taught in Africa. Doug is married with three grown children. Whether speaking, writing, or in conversation, his desire is to come alongside others to help facilitate their alignment with God.

Why Disciplines?

He went down with [his parents] and came to Nazareth, and was obedient to them . . . and Jesus increased in wisdom and in years, and in divine and human favor.

Luke 2:51-52, NRSV

As a part of my formal education, I was required to write a dissertation—a very long and detailed book based on my research. This document consisted of five chapters and almost three hundred pages, a work of which I feel proud. I am not so proud, however, of how long it took me to write it—five years. There are many reasons I can cite to account for why it took that long—I was working full-time, married with three young children, etc. But a major reason was that until the final year-and-a-half, I did not have a good writing discipline. My goal was clear—to finish writing the dissertation and successfully defend it—and I possessed a strong desire to achieve that goal, but for too long I lacked the means for reaching that goal. It finally came down to saying "no" to some daily and weekly schedule commitments so that I could say "yes" to writing during regularly scheduled blocks of time at a designated writing location. In other words, it took discipline.

Reflect on this . . .

What do you desire most in life?

What are your major goals?

What frustrates your desires and keeps you from achieving your goals?

Discipline is necessary to realize our desires and goals. It is a means to an end, a method for moving forward, a path toward a destination, a way of living that enables accomplishment. If you have a goal of any kind, you will need discipline to realize that goal.

Of our many desires and goals, this study focuses on the Christian's yearning for deeper life in God and more faithful living out of faith in Jesus Christ. The apostle Paul describes the yearning this way:

> "I consider everything a loss because of the surpassing worth of knowing Christ Jesus my Lord . . . I want to know Christ—yes, to know the power of his resurrection and participation in his sufferings, becoming like him . . . Forgetting what is behind and straining toward what is ahead, I press on toward the goal to win the prize for which God has called me heavenward in Christ Jesus" (Philippians 3:8, 10, 13-14).

Like Paul, your desire and goal as a Christian can be stated in terms of relationship with God: knowing Jesus, sharing in His life and death, responding to God's call.

This deeper relationship with God is expressed in two interrelated ways, as Jesus pointed out and modeled: "Love the Lord your God with all your heart and with all your soul and with all your mind and with all your strength . . . [and] love your neighbor as yourself" (Mark 12:30-31). Loving God with one's whole self and loving one's neighbor as oneself—this is the end toward which all of the Christian life moves. John Wesley, the great eighteenth century preacher, church leader, and practical theologian summarized it beautifully as: "the humble, patient, gentle love of God and our neighbor, ruling our tempers, words and actions."[1]

Reflect on this . . .

What have you been taught is the purpose and goal of the Christian life?

In what ways does your Christian living demonstrate relationship with God? Love?

Why are disciplines necessary for a Christian to love God with one's whole self and one's neighbor as oneself? Consider these reasons:

1. **GOD WANTS OUR COOPERATION WITH THE WORK BEGUN ON OUR BEHALF.** Loving God and neighbor requires the work of God's grace. Only God's great love active in us can enable the response of love in return to God and to other human beings. The Holy Spirit, by communicating God's love to us and by continually inviting us to respond in love to God and to others, increases our capacity to love God with our whole self and our neighbor as ourselves. Increased capacity to love in this way is not something we can accomplish on our own but neither does it occur naturally or automatically when we open our heart to the work of the Holy Spirit. Increased capacity comes through ongoing, lifelong relationship with God wherein we cooperate with the long, slow work of the Holy Spirit in the midst of our ordinary, daily lives.

   John Wesley referred to the practices where we encounter God and cooperate with the Holy Spirit for the sake of increased capacity to love as "means of grace." In our time they are most often called "spiritual disciplines." Both terms communicate something important—the ultimate significance and goal of the practices are found in God's grace, but they require discipline on our part.

2. **BEING FULLY FORMED INTO THE IMAGE OF CHRIST TAKES TIME AND PATIENCE.** When we receive Jesus into our lives we do not automatically become like Jesus. Although we were created (formed) in God's likeness to love God and all creation, we have been de-formed by the effects of sin. That de-forming work needs to be reversed and, although our lives may be radically and miraculously turned around to a new direction of following Christ, we follow as de-formed humans.

Our openness and surrender to God in conversion and sanctification experiences put us in position to be made more like Christ, but the actual work of conforming to that image—a work known as spiritual formation—follows those experiences in the form of disciplined living.

God wants a lifelong relationship with us. The disciplines keep us connected to God in this relationship, forming and shaping us into Christlikeness over the long haul.

3. **SPIRITUAL GROWTH TAKES PLACE IN BODIES.** Loving God and loving our neighbor take shape in the concrete practices of ordinary, human life and in and through our very human flesh-and-blood bodies. We see this most vividly in Jesus. Accordingly, each chapter in this book begins with a Gospel verse illustrating Jesus' embodied spirituality. Contrary to the teaching of some spiritual traditions, Christianity affirms that there is no separation between the spiritual and the physical. Disciplines are necessary in the Christian life because bodies require discipline to serve purposes higher than mere self-fulfillment. Ask an athlete.[2]

Reflect on this . . .

Of the three reasons given above for the necessity of Christian disciplines, which do you find most compelling? Explain.

Which reason most challenges your current lifestyle? How?

What other reasons would you add to the list based on your experience with disciplines?

The apostle Paul recognized the value of bodily discipline when he wrote to the Christians at Corinth, pointing out that:

"Everyone who competes in the games goes into strict training. They do it to get a crown that will not last, but we do it to get a crown that will last forever. Therefore I do not run like someone running aimlessly; I do not fight like a boxer beating the air. No, I strike a blow to my body and make it my slave so that after I have preached to others, I myself will not be disqualified for the prize" (1 Corinthians 9:25-27).

We, together, are the body of Christ (1 Corinthians 12). Self-discipline often benefits the well-being of a community, contributing to the common good. Ask a soldier.[3] Spiritual disciplines enable Christians to live their faith in their bodies for the sake of the well-being of others' bodies, including the body of Christ, the Church.

We often use the language of discipleship to describe what it means to be a Christian. If our desire and goal is to be disciples, then discipline is a means to that end. It is not an accident that the two words are related—it takes discipline to be a disciple. Jesus told His disciples: "Whoever wants to be my disciple must deny themselves and take up their cross and follow me" (Mark 8:34). The purpose of this study is to map out and offer you initial guidance for how to, in daily life, deny yourself, take up your cross, and follow Jesus.

it takes *discipline* to be a *disciple*...

Each of the following chapters focuses on a specific discipline that functions as an important means of grace in the Christian life. Each discipline contributes to the transformation of heart and life, enabling increased capacity to love God and neighbor as Jesus has taught us. Each discipline uniquely shapes (forms) us to love and enables (empowers) us to love.

Chapter	Discipline	Shapes	Enables
Two	Reading	*Story*	*Perspective*
Three	Praying	*Speech*	*Honesty*
Four	Connecting	*Vision*	*Humility*
Five	Fasting	*Appetite*	*Self-control*
Six	Giving	*Attitude*	*Generosity*
Seven	Receiving	*Posture*	*Trust*

NOTES:

2

Reading

Shaping Story and Enabling Perspective

Jesus went to Nazareth, where he had been brought up, and on the Sabbath day he went into the synagogue, as was his custom. He stood up to read.

Luke 2:51-52, NRSV

Jesus was a Jew and, as such, belonged to a "people of the book." Christians and Jews have been given this label for good reason. Each of these faiths is based on a revelation through a sacred book, and followers of each tradition are expected to read or be read to from that book. For Christians, the book is the Old and New Testaments which together form our Bible.[4]

Is reading really a necessary Christian discipline? After all, some people have difficulty reading or can't read at all. What about the illiterate and those who do not have access to books? It is true that many people of faith in the past have not had access to the book we call the Bible and that many could not have read it even if they had a copy. The same is true today in many parts of our world. But the reason we are people of the Book is that, first and foremost, we are people of "the story." This story is God's story of salvation. The Bible recounts this story as it has been expressed and responded to (Romans 10:17) by people across many centuries and across many cultures. This is an invaluable resource for Christians today. We, today, need to know and be reminded of God's story of salvation, so that it can become our story of salvation.

All people, whether or not they can read books, have and tell stories. Sometimes we read stories and other times we have them read to us. There are family stories, ancestor stories, ethnic stories, national stories, and deeply personal stories. Together these stories form and shape our identity—who we are and who we hope to become. If our most basic identity, however, is Christian—a follower of Jesus Christ whose goal is to become like Christ—these stories will not by themselves be sufficient. We need a bigger story than the stories of our individual, family, ethnic and national stories. We need the story of God's activity in the world across time and place. The Bible provides this. The first verse of Genesis, "In the beginning God created" (Genesis 1:1), and the first verse of John, "In the beginning was the Word" (John 1:1), resonate with that familiar line from our childhood storybooks, "Once upon a time." They link God's actions from the beginning with speaking, and books, after all, are recorded speech.

Reflect on this . . .

What have been your most positive and negative experiences of reading?

How do stories function in your family and/or cultural group?

"The Bible is God's story"—how does this claim match up with your understanding of the Bible? How does God's story in Scripture affect your life story?

Reading the Bible is an indispensable practice for Christians because God's story is not simply one story to be set alongside the other stories of our lives. It is the story that can shape our experience and understanding of all other stories. Why read the Bible? Because, as you do, it will re-shape and transform your personal story, your family story, your ethnic story, and your national story. These other stories can lead to a restricted self-, family-, ethno-, or national-centric life. The Scriptures can liberate you from these restrictions to see yourself, your family, your ethnic group, and your nation from the perspective of God's "bigger picture."

Reading the Bible is an indispensable practice for Christians

This is what reading enables: perspective. This is true of all reading, not just the Bible. When I read, I enter into the world of the author which may be (and most often is) a quite different world than the one in which I live. The good news is that spending time in this other world gives me new perspective on my world. I see my present circumstances with new eyes.

Reading for perspective, however, is a discipline. Why?

1. **READING TAKES EFFORT.** Whether in print book form, electronically formatted, or an audio version, the challenge is the same—making the effort to read or be read to from Scripture in a regular, sustained way over time.
2. **READING REQUIRES FOCUS.** While some reading may be for pleasure, most reading-for-perspective is work. Reading the Bible carefully and attentively is important work for the Christian but requires focused time and energy.
3. **READING TAKES COURAGE.** It has been said that reading is one of the most dangerous, subversive activities in which one can engage.[5] Reading-for-perspective opens my mind and heart to be changed by what I read and to act accordingly. Nothing could be more radical and therefore require more courage than reading God's Word with openness to the Holy Spirit for personal transformation and social action.

Reflect on this . . .

What is your biggest challenge in reading?

Do you read the Bible in a disciplined way? Why or why not?

What are some areas of your life that need to change and how might reading Scripture help bring about these transformations?

Since reading the Bible (and other spiritual texts) is a discipline, we can use help.

Dietrich Bonhoeffer, a twentieth-century German Lutheran pastor and theologian martyred in a Nazi concentration camp, made a helpful distinction between two approaches to Bible reading.[6] Each is a different discipline, but both are necessary for the Christian. The first is individual Bible reading for devotions. This typically consists of reading brief, selected texts (the choice often made for personal reasons) accompanied by prayers to personally apply the Word to my life (that is, my personal story). The second is communal Bible reading for small groups or public worship. This should consist of lengthier, continuous readings from the entire Old and New Testaments (the choice made systematically) with the goal of hearing the whole story of God and the big picture of God's work in the world. Communal reading of the Bible is accompanied by prayers for the well-being of the Christian fellowship and for the whole world.

John Wesley offered practical advice for spiritual reading, condensed into five recommendations[7]:

1. ***Assign a designated time every day for reading and observe it as best you can.*** Like other important things in our lives—work, church attendance, family time, exercise—spiritual reading must be scheduled.
2. ***Begin a time of reading by first declaring your intention to God in prayer.*** Because spiritual reading is a relational exercise, it is important to acknowledge the relationship up front. Ask God to speak to you through the reading, that the Spirit would make it God's Word to and for you.
3. ***Read slowly, seriously, and with great attention, giving space for reflection, the enlightening work of divine grace, and application to life.*** For the most part our culture values doing as much as possible as quickly as possible. Reading the Bible as a spiritual discipline requires you to be countercultural in this respect. The reading is not the goal in itself; it is a means for opening up communication from and with the God who speaks through the Word.
4. ***Allow the reading to affect your senses and feelings, stirring you to prayer and to memorize those passages that engage you.*** Jesus calls

us to love God with every part of us, all of our humanity. Sometimes we view reading as an intellectual exercise that only engages our critical thinking. To the contrary, reading-for-perspective involves the use of our imagination and our senses, including the "felt sense" of what the reading stirs in us.

5. ***Conclude a time of reading with a brief prayer asking God to bring fruit from the seeds planted.*** Regardless of where your reading has taken you (even if it seems like "nowhere"), end it as you began with an affirmation of your personal relationship with God. Only the same Spirit that inspired the Scriptures to be the Word of God can use them to transform our lives into the image of Christ.

Reflect on this . . .

Of the practical resources and suggestions above, which one or two will you adopt to help your reading discipline?

What communal reading discipline might be most helpful for your church community to adopt, so that "the word of Christ [will] dwell in you richly" (Colossians 3:16)?

NOTES:

3

Praying

Shaping Speech and Enabling Honesty

About three in the afternoon Jesus cried out in a loud voice, “My God, my God, why have you forsaken me?”

Matthew 27:46

The previous chapter emphasized the Scriptures as God's story. Reading and being read to from the Bible creates the opportunity for it to become God's Word to us, shaping our story. But shaping the story of our lives doesn't happen automatically. Because Christian discipleship is (and therefore, Christian disciplines are) based in relationship to God, there is a second discipline that goes hand in hand with reading: praying. The relationship begins with God—God speaks first. The relationship continues with our response—we speak back.

Prayer is speech offered to God in response to God's speaking to us. Prayer begins—not with us, but with God. God prays in us; as we join in, the praying becomes ours as well. We carry a false and unnecessary weight of responsibility when we assume that prayer only happens if we initiate it. To the contrary, God's Spirit is active with our spirit constantly, praying within us, breathing out the very life and desires of God. Paul, in his letter to the Romans, put it this way: "In the same way, the Spirit helps us in our weakness. We do not know what we ought to pray for, but the Spirit himself intercedes for us through wordless groans. And he who searches our hearts knows the mind of the Spirit, because the Spirit intercedes for God's people in accordance with the will of God" (Romans 8:26-27). John Wesley called this "prevenient grace," the grace that comes before our response.

Prayer begins—not with us, but with God.

Nonetheless, Christians sometimes find praying feeling like work and a prayer life difficult to sustain. Why is this so? If we do not need to initiate or create prayer (God does that), then why is praying a discipline? Praying requires discipline because responding to God can be difficult work. Consider how this is true in human relationships. A good friend sends me a message that is both personally revealing and affirming of our relationship. I am grateful for the initiative shown by my friend and the reminder that this friendship is mutual. Now the ball is in my court. It is my turn to respond with a reply message. Taking the time to do this is not always easy and crafting the response may feel like work. But I will do it for the sake of the relationship. Failure to engage the discipline of responsive communication would jeopardize the friendship.

Reflect on this . . .

What have been your most positive and negative experiences of praying?

If God's role is to initiate praying, what is your role as a pray-er?

What do you find most difficult or challenging about responding to God in prayer?

Our personal and communal prayer response to God can take different forms:

1. **WORDS.** When Jesus taught His disciples to pray, He said "When you pray, say . . ." (Luke 11:2). Sometimes the words we say or write are spontaneous expressions of our thoughts or feelings, but we also use words that have been provided for us. Examples include the words of Scripture (e.g., the Lord's Prayer), written prayers of the saints of the Church (e.g., the Prayer of St. Francis, "Lord, make me an instrument of your peace . . ."[8]), or prayers that have been handed down to us by our family or congregation (e.g., "Lord, bless this food to our body's use"). These words are great gifts to us and should be used often in public worship and private devotion. The words of others' prayers can help shape our own so that our speech, whether we are formally praying or not, is more faithful to God's speech.
2. **BODY LANGUAGE.** Babies do not need words to effectively communicate. So, too, in our praying, there are times when words are not necessary, for example during great suffering or great celebration. A sigh, tears, moaning and groaning, an upward glance, a tightened fist, loud yelling—these are bodily ways of expressing deep desire and feeling (positive or negative). Sometimes these expressions capture who we are and what we are experiencing better than words. As such, they allow us to bring more of ourselves to God in prayer. The psalmist confessed: "I am feeble and utterly crushed; I groan in anguish of heart. All my longings lie open before you, Lord; my sighing is not hidden from you. My heart pounds, my strength fails me; even the light has gone from my eyes" (Psalm 38:8-10). God hears, understands, and welcomes these honest expressions.

3. **BEAUTY.** The mediums of music, art, and other creative ventures can become expressions of prayer, as Christians throughout the centuries have discovered and practiced. This is true whether we mediate on God's beauty in creation or, as co-creators with God, create the beauty ourselves. We pray when we acknowledge the Creator in the created, the Beautiful One in the beauty, the Spirit at work in the labor (2 Kings 3:15). For, indeed, God fills us "with the Spirit of God, with wisdom, with understanding, with knowledge and with all kinds of skills—to make artistic designs for work in gold, silver and bronze, to cut and set stones, to work in wood, and to engage in all kinds of crafts" (Exodus 31:3-5).[9]

4. **SILENCE.** There are times when doing anything—speaking words, groaning, or creating beauty—is inadequate to express the speech of our soul to God. Like Jesus as He approached the momentous event of His crucifixion in Jerusalem, we too are invited to keep silent (Mark 14:61; cf. Isaiah 53:7), to "be still and know that I am God" (Psalm 46:10). Silence before God in humility and reverence, open to receive whatever it is that God has for us, is perhaps the most basic and important of all prayer postures. It signals loving surrender to God. By moving past the pretense of words and actions, many of which are self-justifying, we place ourselves honestly and vulnerably before God, as we are. No agenda. Simply present (cf. Psalm 131:2).

Reflect on this . . .

Of the different expressions of prayer, which best fits your personality and experience?

Which expression is most lacking in your personal life, and how might that limit spiritual formation?

Which expression is most lacking in your church life, and how might that be improved?

So that you might, as Paul admonished, "pray continually" (1 Thessalonians 5:17), that is pray faithfully without giving it up as a practice, I recommend the following prayer disciplines:

1. ***Show up.*** As in any significant relationship—a friendship, a marriage, tutoring—this is the most basic discipline. When it comes to praying, the most important thing we can do is show up. When the church gathers to pray, be there. When it is time for your morning or midday or evening personal devotion, be there. When you become aware of a spontaneous movement of God's Spirit in your life, be there. What happens during the prayer time is important, but secondary.
2. ***Pray Scripture.*** Mix reading the Bible with your prayer practice so that your speech is shaped by God's speech. Pray the Psalms especially—all of them. They reference a wide range of life situations, contain the broadest scope of emotional expression, and thereby encourage honesty before God. Memorize and pray the Lord's Prayer regularly, letting its structure be the pattern for all of your praying. Utilize *lectio divina,* a time-tested and simple resource for prayerfully praying the Scriptures.[10]
3. ***Pray at all times and in all situations*** (cf. Ephesians 6:18). We cannot and need not pray the same way always. John Wesley collected and published prayers for use by believers of his day with the intention of "First, to have forms of prayer for every day in the week, each of which contained something of deprecation [confession], petition, thanksgiving, and intercession."[11] Some prayers were appropriate for times of "religious rejoicing," others for times of "religious mourning,"[12] and others for times of "self-examination."[13] The discipline of praying a range of prayers appropriate for the range of life experience expands our life in Christ and our presence in and for the world.

4. ***Pray with and for others.*** We learn to pray by hearing and observing others pray and accompanying each other in the process of learning. Pray with family members, pray in a small group of trusted friends, and pray in the public services of the gathered church. Praying vitally connects us with the world beyond our prayer closet. Find more about the outward movement of the God who is with us in the next Chapter (Four) where we examine the discipline of connecting.

Reflect on this . . .

Of the recommended suggestions above, which one or two will you adopt to help your praying discipline?

How might you more intentionally involve others—family, friends, your local church—in your prayer practice?

4

Connecting

Shaping Vision and Enabling Humility

The Samaritan woman said to him, "You are a Jew and I am a Samaritan woman. How can you ask me for a drink?" (For Jews do not associate with Samaritans.) Jesus answered her, "If you knew the gift of God and who it is that asks you for a drink, you would have asked him and he would have given you living water."

John 4:9-10

The apostle Paul prayed that the first Christians would grow up into Christ together. By using "the Body of Christ" as a primary image, he emphasizes the connection among the various parts (Romans 12:5; Ephesians 4:16). This is because the threat of disconnection was ever present. Consider the following examples from Scripture: They dismissed children as not important enough for Jesus (Matthew 19:13-14); asked Jesus for positions of honor above their fellows (Mark 10:35-40); denied knowing Jesus (Luke 22:54-57); excluded some from the common meal (1 Corinthians 11:17-22); and gave up meeting together (Hebrews 10:25).

The pattern in these stories is the same: a human tendency to exclude others, shrinking one's circle of interaction in contrast to Jesus' call to include others, continually expanding one's circle of interaction. Why, in spite of Jesus' example and command, do we tend to exclude others, disconnecting ourselves from them?

The root of disconnection is the sin of selfishness or pride (cf. the Genesis 3 account of the first sin). We conclude that we want what we want, we do not need others in our life, and so we do not want to be bound to anyone else. Becoming more independent is a normal part of growing up, but in the context of individualistic cultures like those in North America and Europe, independence often becomes unhealthy for individuals and for communities. John Wesley warned that "Christianity is essentially a social religion, and . . . to turn it into a solitary one is to destroy it."[14]

Reflect on this . . .

What are some examples of "disconnecting" that you have experienced or observed?

What challenges do you face personally and culturally in trying to connect with others?

By contrast, the mature Christian disciple might best be described as interdependent. Expanding our circles of interaction to include others more diverse increases our capacity for loving God and neighbor. As John Wesley taught, only "love filling the heart, taking up the whole capacity of the soul"[15] can replace sinful selfishness or pride. This love is received by grace as we faithfully respond to God's invitations to love real flesh-and-blood people in our family, our community, and our world. Expanding our circles of connection becomes the laboratory wherein God expands our capacity to love, not only our neighbor, but God too.[16]

The connection between love of God and love of human beings is a necessary one (1 John 4:20-21). Connecting to others shapes our vision of God. When I am disconnected from others, God becomes not much more than an extension of me and my immediate, preferred community, a projection of my/our needs, wants, and concerns. My limited view of God, in turn, cramps my capacity to love God for who God truly is, and reinforces my unloving behaviors toward fellow human beings. However, when I connect with others in increasingly expanding circles, God is revealed in new splendor and beauty, and with new challenges for me to grow in Christlikeness. I learn that God is not my gender, my skin color, my nationality, my language, my socio-economic-political preferences. God is always much more. Freed from selfishness and pride, I can more freely love God and others for who they truly are because I see them more clearly. Loving in this way is a very concrete, practical expression of being like Jesus who, in His time on earth, was known as one who spent time with those looked down upon (Mark 2:15-17).

Expanding our circles of connection becomes the laboratory wherein God expands our capacity to love.

Reflect on this . . .

Share a story with someone of how connecting with others has helped you to grow as a Christian.

How might ever-widening circles of interaction enable you to know and understand God in a deeper and richer way?

It can be fairly easy to connect with those who are like us, who like us, and who can advance our personal agendas. Love is not necessary. On the other hand, expanding our circles to include those not like us, those who do not like us, and with whom relationship will not likely advantage us, does require love.

Connecting is a discipline, involving intention and hard work to expand one's circle of interaction. Consider these ever-expanding circles of potential interaction for you as a Jesus follower. Each is an expression of "neighbor" and calls for the discipline of connecting:

1. **LOCAL CHURCH WORSHIP GATHERINGS.** The apparent weakness of the church—it is a collection of mostly insignificant folk who otherwise would not join together—is actually its strength. Even the smallest congregation is made up of diverse people, each uniquely reflecting the image of God. Christian worship is most spiritually formative when the gathering expands your circle of interaction beyond your own types and preferences.
2. **ACCOUNTABILITY MEETINGS.** John Wesley, although highly successful in attracting large crowds of people to preaching services, recognized that believers can only mature as disciples of Jesus when they know well and are known well by others on the journey of faith. Therefore he tirelessly encouraged all Christians to connect with others for the purpose of accountability in Christian life and mission.
3. **OTHER CHRISTIAN GROUPS.** While rooted deeply in and committed to your own branch of the Christian family tree, there is much to learn from other Christian groups who because of their unique history and calling have developed practices that can enrich your own disciplines.[17] Love expressed between and among differing Christian groups is itself a witness to those outside the Church who, after all, will know we are Christians by our love for one another (John 13:35; 1 John 4:12).

4. **YOUR SURROUNDING COMMUNITY AND WORKPLACE.** Outside the family of Christian faith are many with whom you may connect and by so doing learn how to more fully love God and neighbor (those with whom you live and work, people in your neighborhood, and the local community of which you are a part). It takes discipline to prayerfully and intentionally connect and share Jesus with people who may have a different skin color, speak a different language, live on the other side of town (especially if it has a reputation as a place to avoid), or practice a different religion (or no religion at all).

5. **THE WORLD BEYOND YOUR BORDERS.** Jesus said in what is often referred to as the Great Commission, "Go and make disciples of all nations, baptizing them in the name of the Father and of the Son and of the Holy Spirit, and teaching them to obey everything I have commanded you" (Matthew 28:19-20). Making disciples refers to the one who goes as well as those to whom one goes. You will be made (spiritually formed) into a more mature disciple when you connect with others who live in worlds beyond your borders, whether they are local, regional, national, ethnic, economic, or religious borders.

6. **YOUR ENEMIES.** In considering the above categories, you may have already thought about people you do not like and who do not like you. Identifying our enemies as neighbors—perhaps the most challenging form of connecting Christians are called to do—is important because both Jesus (Matthew 5:43-44) and Paul (Romans 12:19-20) did. Only by connecting with your enemies, not to fight them but to seek their well-being, can you learn how to forgive—the hallmark of the Gospel message.

Reflect on this . . .

If the Good Samaritan parable were to be re-told in your context, what people group(s) might substitute for "Samaritan"?

Of the different circles of interaction above, which one or two will you make a focus for your connecting discipline?

How might your church help you to connect with more diverse others?

As you expand your circles of interaction, your vision of God and the world will be shaped, enabling you to be more humble about yourself and your place in God's vast, wonderful world. Increased humility gained from loving your neighbors makes you more usable by God (James 4:10) for God's purposes.

NOTES:

5

Fasting

Shaping Appetite and Enabling Self-Control

Jesus was led by the Spirit into the wilderness to be tempted by the devil. After fasting forty days and forty nights, he was hungry.

Matthew 4:1-2

Of the disciplines for Christian living, many believers experience fasting as particularly difficult and unsatisfying. Even relatively successful attempts to practice it may not answer the question, "Why fast?" This is a very important question, but before answering it, I invite you to consider reasons why the practice is so difficult.

1. **IT IS COUNTERINTUITIVE, EVEN ILLOGICAL.** Our natural bodily response to feeling hungry is to eat, or when thirsty to drink. To deliberately deny ourselves when food and drink are readily available doesn't make sense to our normal way of operating.
2. **IT HURTS.** When we fast we feel the pain physically which, in turn, puts stress on our mental and emotional state.
3. **IT IS COUNTERCULTURAL.** Consumer cultures by definition teach that more is better. Fasting by definition reduces consumption.
4. **IT THREATENS EGO.** Denying ourselves anything raises the specter of harming ourselves, making ourselves weak, leading us toward death. Instinctually, we want to not only survive, but thrive, ensuring our place in the world.

Perhaps you can already see why fasting is so important for a Christian, even though it is difficult and often not satisfying. The goal of the Christian life is to deepen our capacity to love God and neighbor and therefore must involve more than just attending to our own needs and desires. All of the Christian disciplines help move us beyond just living for ourselves, but fasting is particularly helpful because it challenges self-serving love at the most basic

Reflect on this . . .

Share a story about an experience you had with fasting.

What do you find most difficult & challenging about fasting?

Why should Christians fast?

level of our bodily appetites. In short, it brings us back to God (Joel 2:12), moving us toward confession of our sin and the "repentance that leads to salvation and leaves no regret" (2 Corinthians 7:10).[18]

To put it bluntly, "If we cannot control our appetites, it is unlikely that we can ever be strong enough to give up anything for the sake of another when it runs counter to one of our appetites. Loving our neighbor as ourselves will always be out of our reach."[19] I fast, therefore, so that by saying NO to something, I might have greater freedom to say YES to something even more important; for example, acting lovingly toward another. So here is a working definition: fasting is temporarily or permanently saying NO to an appetite so that you might with more focus and energy say YES to the desire to love God and neighbor. As a means of grace, fasting yields the fruit of the Spirit named "self-control" (Galatians 5:23). Increased self-control enables the Holy Spirit to work in and through you more freely to do what is right (live righteously) for the sake of others.[20]

fasting yields the fruit of the Spirit named "self-control"

When you fast you deny yourself something that is good. Refraining from murder is not fasting, nor is avoiding any other sin. Rather, fasting acknowledges the goodness of that which is denied—food, drink, sex, entertainment, information, power—and reinforces that goodness by refusing to serve it as a god. Fasting reaffirms God as the ultimate Good Creator and Provider. Everything that God made derives its goodness from God, including us. Fasting reminds us, as God's creatures, of our proper relationships in the created order—lovingly trusting God as Heavenly Father and humbly caring for the rest of God's creation.

Most fasting is a temporary self-denial. Fasting from food and drink—the most common form of fasting—must be or else one faces certain death. Other temporary forms of fasting, for example from certain media, from married sexual pleasures, or from purchases, serve the same purpose. Each in its own way helps Christians shape their natural appetites to serve their appetite for God.

Some Christians—the tradition calls them "ascetics"—are called to a unique form of fasting in which they covenant to permanently deny satisfying a particular appetite for the sake of forging a focused, lifelong path of devotion to God and the world God loves.[21] Examples include celibates, vegetarians, and those living in voluntary poverty. As individuals and in community, ascetics have been important witnesses to the radical claims of the Gospel throughout the church's history and continue to be so today. Not all Christians are called to be ascetics in this sense; nonetheless, all Christians are called to some temporary ascetic practices in order to be

Reflect on this . . .

Describe a situation where saying NO to something enabled an important YES. What happens when we base our faith on saying NOs without corresponding YESs?

What did Jesus mean when He said that "Whoever wants to be my disciple must deny themselves and take up their cross and follow me" (Mark 8:34)?

What makes the difference between a healthy and an unhealthy form of self-denial?

formed into the image of Christ. Classic and contemporary disciplines of fasting are a primary means to this end.

How can you practice fasting toward this end? Consider these suggestions:

1. ***Catalog your appetites.*** All humans have similar appetites, but they vary in strength and frequency. What are your strongest natural appetites (food, drink, sex, power, attention from others, media distraction, spending)? Over which do you have the least self-control? Which appetites, when catered to, tend to weaken your appetite for God

and God's work in the world? Make these the starting place for your fasting practice.

2. ***Examine your motives.*** Christian disciplines can be engaged for the wrong reasons. Jesus warned those who would fast not to be hypocritical by making it a self-improvement project or a show for others (Matthew 6:16). Keep the focus on loving God and entering more freely into God's mission in the world. "Is not this the kind of fasting I have chosen," says God through the prophet Isaiah: "to loose the chains of injustice and untie the cords of the yoke, to set the oppressed free and break every yoke? Is it not to share your food with the hungry and to provide the poor wanderer with shelter—when you see the naked, to clothe them, and not to turn away from your own flesh and blood?" (Isaiah 58:6-7).

3. ***Start small.*** Because fasting deeply affects the body (especially our brain), it is best to follow the advice given to those beginning a physical exercise regimen. At first, keep your discipline brief and non-strenuous, so that you can listen carefully to your body and gradually adjust the routine so that it strengthens rather than harms you. John Wesley encouraged "several degrees of fasting which cannot hurt your health."[22]

4. ***Do it for the sake of others.*** Fasting is meant to be a connecting practice that strengthens our bond not only with God but with the whole world. When you fast from food, remember those who are continually hungry and malnourished. When you fast from sexual activity, remember those who are alone and rejected. When you fast from speaking, remember those who, because of who they are, have no one who listens or takes them seriously. When you fast from spending money, remember those who do not have adequate shelter or

transportation. In fact, go a step further: combine your fast with acts of charity and work for justice.

5. ***Link it with prayer and accountability.*** The Scriptures almost always link fasting with praying (Mark 9:29), and for good reason. It is not a discipline to be practiced alone. Acknowledge God at the beginning and end, thank God for the gifts of life, intercede for others who are suffering and in need, and ask God to use your self-denial to make you more like Jesus. Whenever possible, join with others to fast and ask for guidance from an experienced mentor. Knowing you are not alone can help you remain faithful when discouraged and provide you with conversation partners for wisdom and guidance in how to make your practice most fruitful.

Reflect on this . . .

What adjustment (if any) will you make to your fasting discipline? Why?

How might you more regularly join with other believers for fasting and link your fasting with service to others?

Jesus, at the feeding of the five thousand, announced that "My food is to do the will of him who sent me and to finish his work" (John 4:34). Fasting makes more space for God in our life which in turn makes more room for joining God's work in the world.

NOTES:

6

Giving

Shaping Attitude and Enabling Generosity

Jesus . . . withdrew by boat privately to a solitary place. Hearing of this, the crowds followed him on foot from the towns. When Jesus landed and saw a large crowd, he had compassion on them and healed their sick.

Matthew 14:13-14

I recently celebrated my birthday on the continent of Africa, over eight thousand miles from home. Although my wife and children were several time zones away, it ranks as one of my most memorable birthdays thanks to the incredible generosity of my African hosts. They welcomed me as if I was a member of their family, taking time to bless me with kind words and giving me gifts that I knew for some required great sacrifice to purchase. Yet what was for me a remarkable display of love was considered by them to be a matter of course. "This is what Christians do," they would say.

One of my favorite ways to describe God—apparently also a favorite of the apostle John—is that God is love. My African friends showed me that Christian love is demonstrated by specific acts of generosity. We take our cue from God: "For God so loved the world that he gave his one and only Son, that whoever believes in him shall not perish but have eternal life" (John 3:16); "And I [Jesus] will ask the Father, and he will give you another advocate to help you and be with you forever—the Spirit of truth" (John 14:16-17, emphases mine).

The Christian doctrine of the Trinity affirms not only that God is three-in-one—Father, Son, and Holy Spirit—but also that they relate in a very generous manner. God gives God, because that is who God is—One who gives of His very being. The apostle Paul followed the Trinity's example in his attitude toward the Christians at Thessalonica: "because we loved you so much, we were delighted to share with you not only the gospel of God but our lives as well" (1 Thessalonians 2:8). What can you offer to others as an authentic expression of your life?

1. **YOUR PRESENCE.** Simply being with another in ordinary ways can be a precious gift. Show up—especially with your physical presence, but also by using the various forms of social media that connect us to others far and near (cf. Romans 1:11-12).

2. **YOUR TIME.** If you, like me, always have more to do with too little time, then make time for others. It is a form of giving that counters the culture of busyness and communicates to others their true worth (cf. Ephesians 5:15-16).

3. **YOUR MONEY AND POSSESSIONS.** You are a steward, a caretaker for the sake of sharing with those in need. In God's eyes, it is not the amount you own that matters; rather, what you do with what you own (cf. Acts 2:44-45).

4. **YOUR ABILITIES.** It is easy to compare our abilities with others and conclude we do not have much to offer. To the contrary, your unique contribution is necessary for your community to be all that God desires. Do what you can, as to the Lord (cf. Romans 12:6-8).

5. **YOUR TESTIMONY.** Words are not always necessary, but they matter, pointing to and helping clarify to others the source and goal of your actions as a Christian. Telling others of your knowledge of and experience with God gives them greater access to the story of God for their own lives (cf. Romans 10:14; 1 Timothy 3:15).

Reflect on this . . .

What do you find it easiest to give? Hardest to give?

Read the Scripture reference for each of the giving practices above. What do you learn from these biblical examples and admonitions?

Generous giving is both an attitude and a behavior. We see the proper attitude most clearly in Jesus "who, being in very nature God, did not consider equality with God something to be used to His own advantage;" and the corresponding proper behavior: "rather, he made himself nothing by taking the very nature of a servant" (Philippians 2:6-7). One of the best ways to cultivate and maintain this attitude is to spend time with generous people who engage in Christlike behaviors.

Generous giving is both an attitude and a behavior.

John Wesley used the phrase *works of mercy* to summarize the giving behaviors that shape us to Christlikeness, actions directed towards serving others: "feeding the hungry, the clothing the naked, the entertaining or assisting the stranger, the visiting those that are sick or in prison, the comforting the afflicted, the instructing the ignorant."[23] *Works of piety,* by contrast, focus on the upbuilding of the household of faith, and include many of the disciplines already considered in previous chapters such as praying, reading Scripture, and fasting.

In comparing these two important aspects of the Christian life, Wesley made the remarkable claim that we "should be more zealous for works of mercy, than even for works of piety."[24] Practically he meant that "whenever . . . one interferes with the other, works of mercy are to be preferred. Even reading, hearing, prayer are to be omitted, or to be postponed, 'at charity's almighty call;' when we are called to relieve the distress of our neighbour, whether in body or soul."[25]

Reflect on this . . .

Make two lists, one of the "works of piety" and another of the "works of mercy" encouraged and practiced in your church. What do you notice as you compare the lists?

What do you think Jesus meant when He said "Truly I tell you, whatever you did for one of the least of these brothers and sisters of mine, you did for me" (Matthew 25:40)?

Think of an example of how a change in your attitude led to a change in behavior. Think of an example of how a change in your behavior led to a change in your attitude.

Are you daunted by the challenge of Christlike giving? Do not be discouraged. Generous living in all its dimensions does not come naturally or easily, and there will always be personal, interpersonal, and societal forces pressuring you toward selfishness. Your heart must be redirected from the world's approach of money and possessions—calculated accumulation—to the Christian approach of giving—joyfully letting go (2 Corinthians 9:7). This attitude of giving that Jesus demonstrated during His time on earth will enable you, over time, to develop a lifestyle of generosity.

Consider these practices for cultivating the attitude and behaviors of giving:

1. ***Pay attention to those you are with.*** I have painfully learned that it is possible to be physically present with those I love but not present to them mentally and emotionally. This is true of you in relationship to other people, groups, or parts of town. Learn to recognize and resist your tendencies to "check out" or multi-task, making room to contemplate others.
2. ***Schedule time for works of mercy.*** Your discretionary time will easily fill with activities, including Christian disciplines, which are not directed toward giving to others. Intentionally build into your schedule time for joining with others to do works of mercy.
3. ***Budget and invest your finances.*** The Christian practice of tithing—giving ten percent of one's income to support the ministries of the church—has its roots in ancient Israel (Malachi 3:10), yet remains a prudent practice for contemporary Christians. It is a foundational discipline in an overall budgeting process that can help ensure that your spending is in line with your stated Christian priorities. Some monies above what you need to live on can be invested and thereby multiplied so that you have even more to give away.[26]
4. ***Prioritize activities that utilize your abilities.*** There will always be more legitimate needs in your church and surrounding community than you will be able to personally address. You cannot and need not say YES to every opportunity to give. Serve God's purposes in the world effectively by practicing the discipline of faithfully saying NO to some things so that you can say YES to those that best utilize your God-given abilities.

5. ***Name God's presence and activity in others' lives.*** You, like most, may not be called to preach. Nonetheless, you can speak words of blessing, grace, and guidance to others in everyday conversation. Listen to others so that you learn how they already encounter God and need God, and then share with them the vocabulary of faith by which they can, in turn, "speak and tell of [God's] deeds, . . . faithfulness and . . . saving help" (Psalm 40:5, 10).

Reflect on this . . .

On which of the above disciplines will you focus to take the next step toward Christlikeness?

Who could you ask for help in learning these disciplines? With whom might you join in a regular giving practice?

We can only give of that which we have received. The good news is that, as Christians, we have received much from God. The even better good news is that we can continue to receive from God.

NOTES:

7

Receiving

Shaping Posture and Enabling Trust

> Jesus came from Galilee to the Jordan to be baptized by John. But John tried to deter him . . . Jesus replied, "Let it be so now; it is proper for us to do this to fulfill all righteousness."
>
> *Matthew 3:13-15*

Each of the disciplines we have considered—reading, praying, connecting, fasting, and giving—has a common built-in danger. In doing them, I might believe that the doing in-and-of-itself in some automatic or magical way accomplishes their intended end. Forgetting God's grace, I assume sole responsibility for my salvation, my sanctification, trusting in the disciplines to make me holy enough to merit God's favor.

To offset this danger, we need a discipline that keeps the others in perspective and our relationship with God in balance. Thankfully, there is such a discipline—receiving—and it returns us to where we began this journey: dependent on God's grace.

As a tall person (six-feet, two-inches) I have a tendency to slouch. Appropriately so, my family often warns me of the dangers of bad physical posture. I find it helpful to think of receiving as a posture also, a relational stance vis-à-vis others, including God. Relational postures range from open to closed, welcoming to rejecting, receptive to defensive, and are most often evident in body language. Contrast, for example, someone greeting you with a warm smile and extended hand with another staring at you with arms crossed.

The relational posture toward God most conducive to ongoing spiritual formation is receiving, as these Scriptures remind us: "Truly I tell you, anyone who will not *receive* the kingdom of God like a little child will never enter it" (Mark 10:15); "Yet to all who did *receive* him, to those who believed in his name, he gave the right to become children of God" (John 1:12); "Out of his fullness we have all *received* grace in place of grace already given" (John 1:16); "And with that he breathed on them and said, '*Receive* the Holy Spirit'" (John 20:22); "Through him we *received* grace and apostleship to call all the Gentiles to the obedience that comes from faith for his name's sake" (Romans 1:5); "Do you not know that your bodies are temples of the Holy

Spirit, who is in you, whom you have *received* from God? You are not your own" (1 Corinthians 6:19); "Let us then approach God's throne of grace with confidence, so that we may *receive* mercy and find grace to help us in our time of need" (Hebrews 4:16, all emphases mine).

Perhaps you have learned a closed posture in your relationship with other human beings. If you have been mistreated or taken advantage of, you are justifiably cautious and careful about exposing yourself to further hurt. If you have been taught to value personal independence, offers of help from others may feel like a threat to your competence. Mistrust of others can make it hard to trust God. Receiving from God, therefore, is an important discipline for helping us to open up and remain open in the face of our tendencies to close up in fear or push away out of self-sufficiency. Receiving God's grace enables further trust in God.

Reflect on this . . .

In your practice, which of the Christian disciplines tend to become disconnected from God's grace? What helps you get them back in proper perspective?

Which do find easier: to give or to receive? Think about a situation that illustrates how receiving involves trust.

Receiving each of the following can help you develop a posture of openness to receive God's grace in all of life:

1. **BAPTISM AND THE LORD'S SUPPER.** Submitting as Jesus did to the sacrament of baptism (Matthew 3:13-15) and as Jesus instructed to the sacrament of the Lord's Supper (1 Corinthians 11:23-26) anchors your identity in God's redeeming and sanctifying work through the church. You have not earned what these sacraments bestow; they are gracious gifts. The Lord's Supper is also called "Eucharist" which means "thanksgiving." *Receive the sacraments of the church with gratitude.*
2. **CREATION.** The waters of baptism and the physical elements of Holy Communion are ordinary matter that, by the power and presence of the Holy Spirit, communicate God's gracious presence. In fact, all "the heavens declare the glory of God; the skies proclaim the work of his hands." (Psalm 19:1). This is why Jesus often instructed His disciples to look around them for signs of God's kingdom (Matthew 6:26; John 4:35). God is at work making the whole creation new (Romans 8:21). *Receive the beauty and bounty of creation with awe and respect.*
3. **THE DAY.** The Incarnation—God becoming flesh in Jesus (John 1:14)—reveals God's power and presence made known in the midst of ordinary daily living. Even your most difficult or discouraging days are not outside the reach of the Holy Spirit (Psalm 118:24; 2 Corinthians 6:2; Hebrews 3:13). *Receive each day as the specific time and place God uses to form you into Christlikeness.*
4. **YOUR HERITAGE.** Your culture(s) and people are a mixed bag of good and bad influences. You can never entirely escape their formative influence, nor should you. Their input, affirmation, and critique can help you become the person God has created you to be (Psalm 16:6; Proverbs 27:17) *Receive important people in your life as instruments of God's voice.*

5. **YOUR BODY AND MIND.** You are (as I am) damaged goods. You have strengths *and* weaknesses, possibilities *and* limitations, giftedness *and* wounds. Nonetheless, God has made you "a little lower than the angels and crowned [you] with glory and honor" (Psalm 8:5), and God's "power is made perfect in weakness" (2 Corinthians 12:9). Resist the temptation to cut yourself off from the least desirable aspects of your bodily and mental functioning. *Receive all of yourself as capable of becoming God's dwelling place, sanctified for God's purposes.*

6. **SILENCE AND SABBATH.** Two areas where you will confront your limitations are speaking and working. Both are good activities, yet can become idols supplanting right relationship with God and neighbor. The psalmist wisely instructed, "Be still, and know that I am God" (Psalm 46:10). Likewise, the writer to the Hebrews reminds us that "there remains, then, a Sabbath-rest for the people of God" (Hebrews 4:9). *Receive rest from words and labor; in so doing you affirm the primacy of God's speech and work.*

7. **DEATH.** The ultimate form of "letting go" is dying, literally and physically. You can join the "cloud of witnesses" (Hebrews 12:1, referring to those in chapter 11), those believers who over the centuries have died well. Publicly they witnessed to the fact that our hope is not in putting off death, but rather in the resurrection from the dead (1 Corinthians 15:20-22). *Receive your death as the gateway to the fullness of resurrection life.*

Reflect on this . . .

Which of the above disciplines will you focus on to increase your capacity to receive grace?

What could your community of faith do to help you and others cultivate a posture of receiving and to enable trust?

Several years ago my wife suffered a serious stroke. Facing significant medical bills and a temporary loss of income, our family was blessed by the incredible generosity of family and friends, including the church. Nonetheless there were times when finances were so tight I was not sure how we were going to make ends meet. On a Sunday morning at church during one of those times as the offering was about to be taken, I held our tithe check in my hand. "Can I afford to give this money away?" I asked myself, debating whether or not to follow through with my original intention. Implied in my deliberation was another more fundamental question: "Can I trust God to provide?" Moments later, when the offering plate reached me, I dropped in the check—a simple act of faith. Yet my action was not to be the most important of that morning, for the collection was followed immediately by the serving of the Lord's Supper. No sooner had I given, then God came right back at me with "the gifts of God for the people of God." God's giving undergirds and overwhelms all our giving.

Reflect on this . . .

What is the next step for you in practicing the Christian disciplines? What resources do you need?

Close this study with a time of silent prayer. Receive God's grace and be thankful.

Perhaps this is why people like John Wesley was so willing to trustingly commit his life to the God revealed in Jesus. Here is a prayer of commitment he commended to his followers. I invite you to pray this as well, trusting yourself to the God of grace and to the means of grace for transformation of heart and life to love of God and neighbor:

I am no longer my own, but yours. Put me to what you will, rank me with whom you will; put me to doing, put me to suffering; let me be employed for you or laid aside for you, exalted for you or brought low for you; let me be full, let me be empty; let me have all things, let me have nothing; I freely and heartily yield all things to your pleasure and disposal. And now, O glorious and blessed God, Father, Son, and Holy Spirit, you are mine, and I am yours. So be it.[27]

NOTES:

1 John Wesley, "Brief Thoughts on Christian Perfection," *The Works of John Wesley* edited by Thomas Jackson 1872 (reproduced Kansas City: Nazarene Publishing House), XI:446; available at: http://wesley.nnu.edu/?id=786. This collection will be cited hereafter as Works (Jackson).

2 "We all have dreams. But in order to make dreams come into reality, it takes an awful lot of determination, dedication, self-discipline, and effort."—Jesse Owens, American athlete, Olympic gold-medalist 1936.

3 "Accepting discipline means that you are learning to place the task of your unit—your team—above your personal desires . . . When you have learned these things, then you will have military discipline—the kind that saves lives."—The Soldier's Guide. U.S. Department of the Army, 1961, 135.

4 The Jewish book is the Hebrew Bible.

5 "Books can be dangerous. The best ones should be labeled 'This could change your life.'"—author & publisher Helen Exley.

6 Dietrich Bonhoeffer, *Life Together: The Classic Exploration of Faith in Community* (New York: HarperSanFrancisco, 1954).

7 John Wesley, "Advice on Spiritual Reading" [Part of the Preface to John Wesley's Abridgment of Thomas à Kempis' Treatise of *The Imitation of Christ*], in Frank Whaling (Ed.), *John and Charles Wesley: Selected Prayers, Hymns, Journal Notes, Sermons, Letters and Treatises*" (New York: Paulist, 1981), 88-89; available at: http://www.patheos.com/blogs/scriptorium/2011/06/how-to-read-a-spiritual-book-wesley. Cf. John Wesley, "Preface to Explanatory Notes Upon the Old Testament," *Works* (Jackson) XIV:253; available at: http://wesley.nnu.edu/john-wesley/john-wesleys-notes-on-the-bible/preface-to-the-old-testament-notes.

8 The full prayer can be found at http://www.prayerguide.org.uk/stfrancis.htm.

9 An easily accessible and helpful guide to praying visually: Sybil MacBeth, *Praying in Color: Drawing a New Path to God* (Brewster, MA: Paraclete, 2007).

10 Visit http://upperroom.org for a helpful guide to *lectio divina* practice.

11 John Wesley, "Preface to A Collection of Forms of Prayer for Every Day in the Week," in *Whaling*, 77.

12 Ibid.

13 John Wesley, "A Scheme of Self-Examination: Used by the First Methodists in Oxford," In *Whaling*, 85-87; available at: http://www.imarc.cc/one_meth/vol-01-no-12.html.

14 John Wesley, Sermon 24 "Upon Our Lord's Sermon on the Mount, IV," *Bicentennial Edition of the Works of John Wesley*, edited by Frank Baker, et. al. (Nashville: Abingdon, 1984ff.), 1:533; available at: http://wesley.nnu.edu/john-wesley/the-sermons-of-john-wesley-1872-edition/sermon-24-upon-our-lords-sermon-on-the-mount-discourse-four. This collection will be cited hereafter as *Works* (Bicentennial).

15 John Wesley, Sermon 43 "The Scripture Way of Salvation," *Works* (Bicentennial), 2:160; available at: http://wesley.nnu.edu/john-wesley/the-sermons-of-john-wesley-1872-edition/sermon-43-the-scripture-way-of-salvation.

16 John Wesley describes a Christian this way: "Above all, remembering that God is love, he is conformed to the same likeness. He is full of love to his neighbor: of universal love, not confined to one sect or party, not restrained to those who agree with him in opinions, or in outward

modes of worship, or to those who are allied to him by blood or recommended by nearness of place. Neither does he love those only that love him, or that are endeared to him by intimacy of acquaintance. But his love resembles that of him whose mercy is over all his works. It soars above all these scanty bounds, embracing neighbors and strangers, friends and enemies; yes, not only the good and gentle but also the froward, the evil and unthankful. For he loves every soul that God has made, every child of man, of whatever place or nation."—"A Plain Account of Genuine Christianity," *Whaling,* 122.

17 Demonstrated wonderfully by Richard Foster in *Streams of Living Water: Celebrating the Great Traditions of Christian Faith* (New York: HarperCollins, 1998).

18 John Wesley identified five reasons for fasting: "sorrow for sin, bodily health, avoidance of excessive consumption, self-punishment (of which scripture and tradition witness, but Wesley is reluctant to stress), and as an aid to prayer."—Henry H. Knight III. *The Presence of God in the Christian Life: John Wesley and the Means of Grace* (Metuchen, NJ: Scarecrow Press, 1992), 120-121, summarizing a section of Wesley's Sermon 27 "Upon Our Lord's Sermon on the Mount, VII," *Works* (Bicentennial), 1:592-611; available at: http://wesley.nnu.edu/john-wesley/the-sermons-of-john-wesley-1872-edition/sermon-27-upon-our-lords-sermon-on-the-mount-discourse-seven.

19 Diogenes Allen, *Spiritual Theology: The Theology of Yesterday for Spiritual Help Today* (Boston: Cowley, 1997), 68.

20 Author/songwriter Michael Card makes this point in his song "Things We Leave Behind."

21 An addiction is an unhealthy pattern of satisfying an appetite that may become the basis for adopting a permanent fast (abstinence). In these cases, professional treatment is often very helpful.

22 John Wesley, "Minutes of Several Conversations," *Works* (Jackson), VIII:316.

23 John Wesley, Sermon 26 "Upon Our Lord's Sermon on the Mount, VI," *Works* (Bicentennial), 1:573; available at: http://wesley.nnu.edu/john-wesley/the-sermons-of-john-wesley-1872-edition/sermon-26-upon-our-lords-sermon-on-the-mount-discourse-six.

24 John Wesley, Sermon 92 "On Zeal," *Works* (Bicentennial), 3:319; available at: http://wesley.nnu.edu/john-wesley/the-sermons-of-john-wesley-1872-edition/sermon-92-on-zeal.

25 Ibid., 314.

26 John Wesley once said that if Christians who "'gain all they can,' and 'save all they can,' will likewise 'give all they can' then, the more they gain, the more they will grow in grace, and the more treasure they will lay up in heaven."—"Thoughts upon Methodism," *Works* (Bicentennial), 9:530; available at: http://www.gbod.org. To counter the dangers inherent in accumulating wealth, working for and saving money are to be governed by two practices: living as simply as possible and giving as much as possible to the poor.

27 John Wesley, "A Service for Such as Would Make or Renew Their Covenant with God [A Modern Adaptation]," *Whaling,* 387; prayer available at: http://www.wesleymem.org.uk/prayer.shtml.

Other Dialog studies also available!

ELEPHANTS IN THE CHURCH

Conversations We Can't Afford to Ignore

Elephants in the Church centers the conversation around the difficult topics of politics, prejudice, addictions, abuse, sexual sin, materialism, and how to create a safe and open atmosphere for conversations within the Church.

PARTICIPANT'S GUIDE ISBN: 978-0-8341- 2979-5

FACILITATOR'S GUIDE ISBN: 978-0-8341-2985-6

TAKE UP YOUR MAT

And Other Miracles from the Gospel of John

The miracles Jesus performed had a definite impact on the lives of those who experienced them and contain a powerful message for those of us living today. *Take Up Your Mat* unpacks seven miracles found in the gospel of John and explores their message in our current context.

PARTICIPANT'S GUIDE ISBN: 978-0-8341-2981-8

FACILITATOR'S GUIDE ISBN: 978-0-8341-2987-0

Available online at DialogSeries.com